PATMOS

The Holy Island of the Apocalypse

EDITIONS
TOUBI'S ®
ΕΚΔΟΣΕΙΣ

Texts: V. KOURTARA, L. XEROUTSIKOU, THEO. M. PROVATAKIS
Photographs: S. BOURBACHAKIS, P. SPYROPOULOS, TH. PROVATAKIS, I.M. CHATZIFOTIS, Archives: M. TOUBIS

Supervision: I.M. CHATZIFOTIS
Artistic Supervision: NORA ANASTASOGLOU
Typesetting, color separation, montage, printing: GRAPHIC ARTS M. TOUBIS A.E.

On the eve, just a little past midnight
"I was in the isle that is called Patmos".
As dawn began to break I found myself in Chora.
The sea, as motionless as metal, made fast the islands all around.

Not one leaf was breathing in the strengthening light.
A completely flawless shell of peace.
I was transfixed by this dominion
and I found that I was whispering: *"Come and See..."*.

George Seferis

*P*atmos, the island of Christianity, art, beauty and tradition. The holy island as it is called by Christians, pilgrims, writers, scholars and travellers. A place of tranquillity and a center of quietude as all those who have lived there and experienced it, all those who have managed to get to know it at first hand, agree. That is why it is called a spiritual arena and a stadium for those contests where belief is honed, the Orthodox faith is forged and personality is hammered out. Because Patmos is not only a spiritual oasis and a powerful magnet where thousands of the Orthodox faithful find repose and salvation. It is not only an island of golden coasts and pebbled beaches that offer you enchanting, unforgettable, violet sunsets that transport you to the land of dreams. It is much more than that, it is the holy place where the heavens opened and God on High was revealed. It is a "living" place, with a soul and character and a real treasure trove of strong Greek tradition and prolific intellectual presence. It is the spiritual eye of the Ecumenical Throne of Constantinople. It is the holy island of Christianity and Hellenism.

Moreover, the three villages, Chora, Skala and Kambos, with their 365 churches it is said, and their thousands of traditional buildings that have sprung forth from the peaceful slopes or picturesque beaches, from the smooth hills or the shores, from the remote coves or wind-lashed peaks, all crowned by the Byzantine buildings of the great Monastery of St. John the Divine and the Holy Cave of the Apocalypse make up in their totality the full gamut of what Patmos has to offer. A paradisical nature that is offered to one like the beating of heavenly wings. The lacy coastline with its golden sand beaches, the picturesque bays and the dream-like shores, call out to both young and old to get to know them, to relish and enjoy them all year round. From April to October the beaches are full of those who want to swim in the sea, or just enjoy themselves, have fun and be at peace. Few other Greek sites have as many natural beauties as Patmos.

The guide book you are holding in your hands endeavors to present, both concisely and collectively, the art, culture, tradition and Orthodox presence on Patmos. In this publication, which has been worked on by various experts with love, zeal and respect, there is a precise and full treatment of what every visitor and every devotee of the beautiful and holy place called Patmos, longs to, and should, know.

THEOCHARIS MICH. PROVATAKIS
Director of the Ministry of Culture

1

PATMOS
The Holy Island
of Christianity
10 - 15

2

NATURE
Site - Sun - Light - Climate
Geomorphology
16 - 19

3

HISTORY
Mythology - Ancient Times - Roman & Byzantine Period
The Contribution of Patmos to the Rebirth of Greece
20 - 25

4

THE HOLY FIGURES OF PATMOS
St. John the Divine - Saint Prochoros
Hosios Christodoulos
26 - 29

5

CULTURE & TRADITION
Inhabitants and Occupations - Architecture - The Patmian School - Easter
The Celebration of the 1900 Years since the Apocalypse
30 - 45

6

THE HOLY APOCALYPSE
The Holy Cave of the Apocalypse - The Monastery -The Side-Chapels
The Message of the Apocalypse to the Modern World
46 - 53

7

THE MONASTERY OF ST. JOHN THE DIVINE
Site - Founding - Architecture - The Main Church
The Side-Chapels - The Library - The Archives - The Museum
54 - 69

8

STROLLING THROUGH CHORA
Churches - Mansions
Squares - Lanes
70 - 79

9

MONASTERIES & HERMITAGES
The Evangelismos Convent - The Zoodochos Pigi Convent
The Convent of Ayia Ayion - The Hermitages
80 - 91

10

THE HARBOR OF SKALA
The Center of the Island
The Largest Settlement on Patmos
92 - 99

11

COUNTRYSIDE & BEACHES
North of Skala
South of Skala
100 - 121

12

SMALL ISLANDS AROUND PATMOS
Petrokaravo - Leipsoi - Arkoi - Agathonisi
Practical Informations
122 - 127

1 PATMOS

One comes upon Patmos lying between the islands of Icaria and Leros as one travels along the coast of Asia Minor in the northeastern Aegean. It seems to rise out of the crystalline waters, just the way the ancient myth says. The island of the Apocalypse, the Holy Island of the Aegean, with its aura of devotion, has become a place of pilgrimage for all Christianity. An island full of religiosity, an air of mystery and tranquil beauty. This is a holy place for contemplation and inner quest, but it is also a place to have a good time. This island knows how to hide its natural charms, reserving them for those who will appreciate and respect them. Its landscape, sometimes peaceful and other times harsh, has high cliffs which thrust up toward the sky. The center of the island is commanded by the impregnable Monastery of St. John the Divine. Built in 1088 A.D. of the local greyish-brown stone, it stands in strong juxtaposition to the dazzling white houses of Dodecanesian architecture which surround it.

An island like no other, Patmos played host to St. John the Evangelist and Theologian, while today it is one of the most important sites of Christianity. The cave where St. John wrote down the Apocalypse, the closing book of the New Testament, as well as the majestic Monastery of St. John the Divine are both unique monuments of Orthodoxy which attract thousands of pilgrims and visitors.

The chapel of Profitis Ilias

The Holy Island of the Aegean

Patmos has kept its own special character, unaltered. Faithful to its religious principles, it welcomes visitors and captivates them from the very first glance with its inexplicable magic. A magic that comes from its Greek Orthodox culture which it has developed and retained for over nine hundred years. Utilizing its rich tradition, Patmos has grown into a unique center of Byzantine and post-Byzantine studies whose fame has spread throughout the world. At the same time it has carefully nurtured its tourist infrastructure so that it can offer its visitors modern amenities without altering the sanctity of the place. This island has two different faces which are harmoniously connected to each other. The one is deeply religious, and centered on the mysterious aspect of the Apocalypse and the supernatural, while the other is the natural one, with its calm, tranquil character, highlighted by picturesque landscapes and crystal-clear water.

In the summer the harbor of Skala is full of sailing ships, yachts and cruise boats. There is always a lively, hospitable, and unique atmosphere on Patmos.

2

NATURE

Site - Sun - Light - Climate
Geomorphology

Patmos, the northernmost island of the Dodecanese, lying between Icaria and Samos to the north, Leipsoi to the east and Leros to the south has already captivated any visitor who has seen its unique shape on the map. It is a narrow band of earth 12.5 km. long which stretches out in the Aegean like a flexible ribbon, allowing the salt water to penetrate deeply inland and create countless bays of all sizes. Its lacy shoreline unfolds enchantingly before you for a total of 65 km. Its narrow body becomes even narrower in the middle where it seems about to split in two.

Present-day Patmos is little different from the copperplates found in the books of travellers from the 19th century. All the elements that go into the landscape indicate the holiness of the place. The soil of Patmos is mountainous, volcanic and rocky for the most part, forming ranges of low mountains and hills rising to steep peaks which gaze up at the sky. Between these hills and the sea there are small verdant valleys which soften the landscape. The island of Selene (the Greek goddess of the Moon) who loved the goddess Artemis fervently, is bathed in light, the light of the life-giving sun which shines nearly all year round. That is why Patmos has a mild and gentle climate even during the winter. During the summer the north winds help keep it cool and pleasant. On the eastern side of the island there are several islets dotting the white-tipped waves of the dark blue Aegean. Contemporary development has respected the architectural tradition of the settlements of Chora and Skala. The Monastery of St. John the Divine has played a very enthusiastic part in this. Important environmental conferences have been held on the island in which experts have participated and pilot cultivation programs have been tried on an experimental basis, turning barren extents of land into feasts of greenery. For the inhabitants of Patmos the protection of nature and the preservation of tradition are some of their most important concerns.

Tranquillity is the island's main feature. Only the bells of the large monastery and the horns of the passenger ships in the harbor break the reigning silence and peace.

Patmos has an area of 34 square kilometers and approximately 3,000 inhabitants. Administratively, for historical reasons, it is a municipality to which the neighboring islets of Arkoi and Marathos are also subject. Ecclesiastically it is subject to the Ecumenical Patriarchate and is a Patriarchal Exarchate, the Exarchos being the abbot of the Monastery of St. John the Divine.

Patmos is connected by steamship to Piraeus (163 nautical miles), and the islands of Leros, Kalymnos, Kos, Rhodes and Samos. It is connected to Athens by plane via Samos and the airport on Leros. Patmos is also connected to Samos by Flying Dolphin hydrofoils.

The highest mountain on the island, Mt. Profitis Ilias, is in its southern part and is 269 meters high.

Patmos has a temperate Mediterranean climate; it is volcanic and rocky and there is little rainfall. The entire island is covered by a thin layer of grass, various shrubs (including heather, and the local atsibides shrub) and a number of trees, both small and large. There are pine, cypress, arbutus, eucalyptus, and tamarisk trees as well as various fruit trees, above all pomegranates.

Citrus trees are cultivated by the inhabitants where the soil is suitable and the conditions are right.

Small gardens and a few vineyards are cultivated near the harbor of Skala and in the small valleys scattered around the island.

Aspri, Koumana, Meloi with Skala to the rear.

3

HISTORY

Mythology - Ancient Times - Roman Period- Byzantine Period - Turkish Occupation - Modern Times

An ancient myth says the island rose from the depths of the sea through the divine powers of Apollo and Zeus and for the sake of the goddess Artemis who fell in love with it seeing it under the light of the moon (Selene). The Sun (Helios) gave it life and made it habitable. It is said that Orestes took refuge here after the murder of his mother Clytaemnestra to save himself from the Furies. The history of the island began a very long time ago when the primitive Greek races, the Carians, Lelegians and the Pelasgians visited it

The goddess Artemis of Braurona, worshipped by the ancient inhabitants of Patmos.

before the 3rd millennium, having colonized the surrounding islands even earlier. The first real inhabitants of the island are thought to have been the Dorians who were followed by the Ionians. For Patmos the period around the 4th century B.C. was of particular importance. The Ionians created a flourishing civilization there. They built the town and its acropolis on Kasteli hill and made it a center of export trade. In the 2nd century A.D. the Romans transformed the island into a place of exile. In 95 A.D. the Apostle John arrived on the island as an exile.

Here was written the holy Book of Revelation and many of the inhabitants were converted to Christianity. From the 6th to the 9th century A.D., Patmos, like the rest of the surrounding islands, was decimated by pirate raids. In the 11th century A.D. the Blessed (Hosios) Christodoulos arrived there, and charmed by the tranquil and unique beauty of the landscape founded the Monastery of St. John the Divine. Despite the constant attacks of Arabs and despite the Turkish occupation the monastery managed to hold on to its privileges. At the end of the 16th century Patmos experienced a new round of prosperity. Shipbuilding and trade flourished. Skala became a major harbor. Storehouses were built and Chora was better fortified. The inhabitants increased. The famed Patmian School was founded where many of the most important Greek men of letters studied. Then came the time for Greece to be liberated from the Turks. Patmos, however, like the rest of the Dodecanese, was, after the Turks, to stay under the domination of the Italians until March 1948 when the Greek flag was officially raised.

Mythology

Patmos, the holy island of the Dodecanese, arose from the sea like Delos, the holy island of the Cyclades.

The island was first called Letois because it was thought to owe its existence to the goddess Artemis, the daughter of Leto. According to mythology, the island had originally lain on the bottom of the sea.

The goddess Artemis was visiting Caria, on the mainland across the way, where there was a temple in her honor on Mt. Latmos. There she met Selene, who casting her light on the sea illuminated the sunken island. Selene constantly exhorted Artemis to raise the island and finally convinced her. To accomplish it, the goddess sought the help of her brother Apollo, who in his turn went to Zeus and thus the island emerged from the sea. Helios (The Sun) dried it off, gave it warmth and life and then the first inhabitants arrived, many of whom came from the environs of Mt. Latmos but some from elsewhere, giving it the name Letois.

According to another version, the name Patmos was derived from Mt. Latmos itself.

Mythology relates that Orestes took refuge on Patmos with a number of people from Argos, when he was hunted by the Furies, and built the first large temple to Artemis there on exactly the same location that Hosios Christodoulos chose when he began to build the Monastery of St. John the Divine in 1088.

Ancient Times

According to the experts, the first inhabitants of the island were the Dorians, who were succeeded by the Ionians. From the 6th to the 4th century B.C., a town and acropolis flourished on Kastelli Hill (above present-day Skala). It had a population of 12-15 thousand inhabitants and there were temples there to Zeus, Apollo, Artemis and Dionysos. Classical writers paid little heed to the island. Thucydides mentions its name, saying that in 428 B.C. a general named Pachis pursued the people of Mytilini "to the island of Patmos".

The Roman Period

Patmos, even though it was on the sea lane that led from Roman to Ephesus, was little more than a place of exile. During the time when John, the disciple of Jesus Christ, was preaching in Ephesus, where he had also founded a church, a persecution of Christians was proclaimed by the Roman emperor Domitian. John himself became a victim of this persecution, and was arrested and exiled to Patmos (95 A.D.). There on the island of his exile, St. John, preaching the word of God, turned quite a few of the pagans into Christians and founded the Church of Patmos. He lived in a cave, later called the "Cave of the Apocalypse" where enlightened by a divine commandment he dictated the text of the Book of Revelation to his disciple Prochoros.

The assassination of Domitian in 96 A.D. meant the end of the persecutions and consequently the end of John's exile, as the new emperor Nerva gave him permission to return to Ephesus and continue with his work.

The religious freedom that prevailed with the edict of Constantine the Great, in the 4th century, contributed to the island becoming a place of pilgrimage.

The island's prosperity lasted till the 7th century when suddenly, with the outbreak of hostilities between Byzantium and the Saracens, the island was plundered and laid waste.

The Holy Monastery of St. John the Divine
and its founder Hosios Christodoulos.
Copperplate 1755.

The Byzantine Period

The island again began to flourish in the 11th century with the arrival of Hosios Christodoulos. He was from Bithynia where he had spent the early years of his ascetic life on one of its mountains (see Chapter 4, p. 28).

In 1088 he founded the Monastery of St. John the Divine. In time the Monastery of St. John earned exceptional privileges and there were many of offerings and gifts. The 12th century was a difficult period for Patmos, because of the constant pirate raids and the meddling of bishops from surrounding areas. Around the end of the century, the island revived because of the good administration of the monastery and the protection afforded it by emperors and patriarchs.

After the first fall of Constantinople, to the Franks in 1204, Patmos was occupied by the Venetians, in 1207. Owing to the intervention of the Pope, the Monastery was not disturbed.

For Patmos, the monastery and the island's inhabitants, piracy was always a terrible scourge.

In order for the monks at the Monastery of St. John to counter the constant threats, they had to forge special relations with the Vatican, Venice and various princes in the West as well as the Knights of St. John on Malta.

Indeed quite a number of documents have survived which attest the strong Papal interest in the monastery. During the Byzantine period the island was administratively subject to Samos and ecclesiastically to the Great Church of Christ.

The Turkish Occupation

The occupation of Patmos, as well as the rest of the Dodecanese, by the Turks lasted from 1523-1912 but was not particularly oppressive. Despite the levying of heavy taxes, the island retained its autonomy.

ΕΙΚΟΝΟΓΡΑΦΙΑ ΤΗΣ ΣΕΒΑΣΜΙΑΣ ΚΑΙ ΒΑΣΙΛΙΚΗΣ ΜΟΝΗΣ ΙΩΑΝΝΟΥ ΤΟΥ ΘΕΟΛΟΓΟΥ ΤΗΣ ΚΑΤΑ ΤΗΝ ΝΗ-
ΣΟΝ ΠΑΤΜΟΝ, ΟΙΚΟΔΟΜΗΘΕΙΣΗΣ ΠΑΡΑ ΤΟΥ ΟΣΙΟΥ ΧΡΙΣΤΟΔΟΥΛΟΥ ΔΙΑ ΧΡΥΣΟΒΟΥΛΛΩΝ ΤΟΥ ΑΕΙ-
ΜΝΗΣΤΟΥ ΒΑΣΙΛΕΩΣ ΑΛΕΞΙΟΥ ΤΟΥ ΚΟΜΝΗΝΟΥ.

The suzerainty of the Turks reduced the number of pirate incursions in the Aegean and lead to the gradual development of maritime trade. Wealth flowed into the island and grand mansions and churches were built.

Later this flourishing economy was brought to a halt. The island was destroyed during an invasion and plundered. The following years were difficult as commerce was in crisis and the population was steadily decreasing.

A new period of development for Patmos started in 1669 with the arrival of many Cretan refugees. In 1713 the Patmian School was founded by the hieromonk (a monk in holy orders) Makarios Kaloyeras, and this was the single most important event to occur on the island in the 18th century.

A watercolor of the island of Patmos.

The harbor of Skala, the Cave of the Apocalypse and the Monastery of St. John the Divine in a copperplate.

Patmian costumes, colored copperplates. National Library - Paris..

Modern Times

On the eve of the Greek War of Independence of 1821, Patmos, through its Patmian School, had become a national and intellectual center, and its inhabitants and their ships would take part in the revolt. Three of the earliest and most illustrious of the insurgents of 1821, the Patriarch of Alexandria, Theophilos, Emmanuel Xanthos and Dimitrios Themelis, were all Patmians.

Theophilos Pangostas came from the large Pangostas family which included many eminent figures, such as Parthenios who founded the Holy Convent of Zoodochos Pigi in 1617. Theophilos, also a graduate of the Patmian School, was in 1805 elected the Patriarch of Alexandria; when he came to Patmos in 1819 he took an active role in the national revolt which he faithfully served. Emmanuel Xanthos, one of the three founders of the Philiki Etaireia (the main Greek revolutionary society), studied at the Patmian School and at the age of 20 travelled as
a merchant to the Balkans and Europe but primarily to Russia, where from 1814 on he spread the Society's message. In 1820 he convinced Alexandros Ypsilantis to assume the leadership of the Philiki Etaireia while he himself offered great services to the rebirth of Greece in 1821. This can be seen in the action of the Supreme Committee of the Revolution which appointed Xanthos "to the highest and most lofty position, superior to any other class or distinction". Dimitrios Themelis, also a graduate of the Patmian School, got his start with trade in the Balkans. He became a member of the Philiki Etaireia and in 1821 undertook the direction of the revolt on the Aegean islands, organizing the local revenue departments. In 1824 he was sworn in as "Assistant", that is, the representative of the island at the National Assembly in Argos. In 1825 he was named General Director "of all the political and military affairs of Western Greece" along with two other freedom fighters. He died in Mesolonghi in 1826 during the siege of the town.

4

HOLY FIGURES OF PATMOS

St. John the Divine - St. Prochoros - Hosios Christodoulos

Two great figures of Orthodoxy, St. John the Divine and the Blessed (Hosios) Christodoulos, the founder of the Monastery of St. John the Divine, have by their passage through the island left their blessing to the following centuries which for Patmos is a most valuable legacy. The third holy figure for the island is St. Prochoros. According to religious tradition, he wrote about the life and the miracles of St. John, following him everywhere.

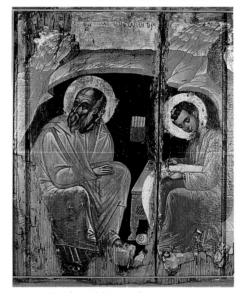

St. John with his disciple, Prochoros.

Christ and are mentioned at all his difficult moments; only they were both present at his Transfiguration, at the miracle of the restoration of the daughter of Jairus and during the praying of the Lord at Gethsemane. John was Jesus' most beloved disciple, to whom he entrusted his Mother when he was put on the Cross. John played an important role in the promulgation of Christianity; he went to Samaria, was particularly active in Palestine along with his brother and Simon Peter and worked at Ephesus.

He wrote the Gospel and his three Epistles there. During Domitian's persecution of the Jews and the Christians (81-96 A.D.) John was exiled on Patmos with his disciple Prochoros, where he wrote The "Book of Revelation" (95 A.D.). He returned to Ephesus after the death of Domitian where he also taught Christianity. He died in 104 A.D. at the age of 99 and was buried at Ephesus.

The Orthodox Church celebrates his memory on 8 May and his metastasis on 26 September. Both of these dates are celebrated at the Holy Monastery of St. John the Divine on Patmos.

St. John the Divine

The written work of St. John the Divine includes "The Gospel According to John", "The Book of Revelation" and three "Epistles". John was a simple fisherman on Lake Tiberius. Together with his brother James, who also became a disciple of Christ, and the future Apostle Peter, he ran a cooperative fishing enterprise. Their father was named Zebedee and their mother Salome. Both John and James had impetuous characters and that is why Christ called them the "sons of thunder". John and Peter were included in the narrow circle of the disciples of

Hosios Christodoulos

Hosios Christodoulos was born in 1021 in Nikaia, Bithynia. He originally lived there as an ascetic, specifically on Mt. Olympos, and then made a pilgrimage to Rome and the Holy Lands (he stayed in the desert of Palestine). Then he went to Asia Minor, to Mt. Latros near Miletus. There he decided to settle near the other ascetics and live as a monk. Later he became the abbot of the Lavra Monastery.

He was forced to abandon that place because of the Saracen raids. So he took refuge on the coast of Asia Minor at Strovilos where Arsenios Skinouris entrusted to him the administration of his monastery, which was located near Halicarnassus. But when the Seljuk Turks arrived there he moved opposite to Kos, where he founded, together with the monks who followed him,

Hosios Christodoulos offering the Holy Monastery.

a monastery in honor of the Mother of God, on Pelion hill and specifically at the site designated by Arsenios Skinouris himself.

The attraction that Patmos exercised on Hosios Christodoulos led him at the beginning of 1088 to Constantinople where he requested the emperor Alexis I Comnenus to let him substitute fertile Kos.for Patmos. The emperor refused at first, but he finally agreed after the intercession of his mother Anna. Through a Gold Bull the emperor ceded absolute suzerainty over the island to Christodoulos.

Hosios Christodoulos was a resilient ascetic, stern, an experienced doctor, a most devout monk and a dynamic founder of monasteries. He arrived at the island accompanied by many educated monks and having in his possession the gold bull that ceded the island to him, as well as an important library. In August 1088 he founded the monastery that he dedicated to St. John the Divine.

The founder of Patmian monasticism obliterated all trace of paganism on the island.

Without having completely finished his work, Hosios Christodoulos was forced yet another time to flee from the island, this time because of pirate raids.

Thus he settled on Euboea where he died on 16 March 1093. Six days before his death he drew up his will, in which he exhorted the monks to carry on the work that he had started on Patmos and to transport his remains to the monastery, and this was done after the cessation of the Turkish raids.

The memory of Hosios Christodoulos is celebrated twice a year on the island. On 16 March (the day of his burial) and 21 October (the day of the removal of his venerable relics).

The Dormition of Hosios Christodoulos.

St. Prochoros

Prochoros was one of the seven deacons ordained by the apostles and later became the bishop of Nicomedia. According to tradition he followed John the Evangelist to Patmos and wrote about his life, his miracles and his apostolic work. Some scholars have raised doubts as to whether he really was a disciple of John, as his name is not mentioned in the ecclesiastical writings of Early Christian times and furthermore his texts contain mistakes and inaccuracies. But other experts maintain that the mistakes are the result of the later copying of the texts. His memory is celebrated on the 28th of June.

St. John the Divine dictating
the Book of Revelation to his disciple Prochoros.
According to tradition, Prochoros also wrote about the life,
the miracles and the apostolic work of John.

CULTURE & TRADITION

Inhabitants & Occupations - Architecture - The Patmian School - Easter - The Celebration of the 1900 Years of the Apocalypse

The cultural tradition of Patmos is undoubtedly much shorter than its religious history: for many centuries the "holy island" was deserted, the way it was when John wrote The Book of Revelation. The first settlements were developed around the end of the 11th century when Hosios Christodoulos began to erect the Monastery of St. John the Divine. With the passage of time, the island's poputation increased significantly due to the existence of the monastery of course, but even more to the refugees from Constantinople, Rhodes and Crete who found a sure refuge on Patmos. This mixing together of different people with different experiences, customs and cultures led to a unique cultural alloy which was of great assistance in the economic, social and intellectual flowering of the island. The crowning point of all this was the founding of the Patmian School, one of the most renowned schools created by Hellenism. But what has always set Patmos apart from all the other islands is its long tradition, the result of its deep religiosity and the faith that rules the lives of all its inhabitants. A tradition that reaches its culmination each Easter when throughout Easter Week there are presentations of stories from the New Testament, spectacular ceremonies in which the faithful take an active part, and other unique customs whose roots are lost in the remote past. Impressive rituals, but at the same time utterly essential experiences which the unique Patmian tradition has kept vital.

The Inhabitants and Their Occupations Today

The permanent inhabitants of the island are involved with farming, fishing and the cultivation of the land on the few suitable areas.

The island is surrounded by hundreds of rocky outcroppings as well as many marine caves, recesses and cavities in rocks where fishermen find abundant fish. Other Patmians exercise the traditional professions of builder, carpenter, beekeeper, tailor of ecclesiastical garments, embroiderer, blacksmith, boat-builder, shepherd and baker while a considerable number of hotels employing local personnel serve the numerous visitors who come mainly during the summer months. Patmos even has charming little shops with all kinds of souvenirs and warm, open-hearted

owners eager to be of help in any way, and recently there has been a very satisfactory development of Byzantine icon painting. Even the row boats and their owners, the caiques and their captains, the picturesque little cafes with fresh hors' d'oeuvres from the sea, the homemade "spoon" sweets and the tasty bread baked for festivals, are all a vital part of the unblemished beauty of the island, along with the traditional buildings and the hotels of Patmos with their modern comforts.

These all form, when taken together, a typically picturesque island full of stories, legends and traditions.

Of course, the island is not lacking in little tavernas with fresh fish and traditional food as well as pastry shops with local sweets. Cozy drinking places have octopus grilling on charcoal, barrelled wine, delicious local bread and the superb Patmian cheese pies, which can be found everywhere.

Architecture

An indispensable feature of Patmian culture, the architecture of Chora has been an important object of study right up to the present, for it is one of the few remaining monuments of Byzantine architecture. The first built nucleus of the island was created at the beginning of the 12th century, with its center at the monastery, which offered security and protection from invasions and pirates. With the passage of the years, the population of the island was augmented by colonists from the surrounding islands, and refugees, but the form of the settlement of Chora remained faithful to urban prototypes and the monastery was firmly at the center. But in 1522, with the occupation of Rhodes by the Turks, the construction of large, free standing mansions began — the first being the Sofouli — at some distance from the fortified zone around the monastery and the settlement began to acquire an agricultural character. The Venetian invasion of Patmos in 1659 weakened the dominance of the monastery once and for all and the subsequent arrival of Cretan refugees (1669) speeded up the changes in the social structure which in its turn had reverberations on architecture: the appearance of the first square, Ayia Levia. From the beginning of the 18th century, there began a rapid development of the town-plan: the urban tissue became denser and settlements that were opposite one another were united, such as Alloteina - Kretika; there was a division of the large properties, and an extension of the fortified zone. In the 19th century the economically and socially powerful Patmos received important influences from neoclassicism, an element that had ideological and ethnic extensions, but which was not in agreement with the building development of the island up to that point. Today, 900 years after the first built nucleus, Patmos, having assimilated and unified the various elements, has still managed to retain its own distinct personality. With but a few isolated exceptions, it is still traditional, impressive and unique.

Built Formations and Art

The culture and the tradition of Patmos are two elements difficult to separate. That is because both of them have their primary source in one unique point: the belief in the existence and the omnipotence of God. The same faith that led Hosios Christodoulos to exchange his land on Kos for the "deserted and uninhabited" Patmos and to build a monastery there in the name of St. John the Divine. The founding of the Monastery of St. John the Divine in 1088 by Hosios Christodoulos had a decisive influence on the built formation of the island. The building of the monastery employed quite a number of people, such as monks, craftsmen, master builders and workers from the surrounding islands.

The first settlement on the island was created around the walls of the monastery by those ordinary people who had settled there with their families. In time, the population of the settlement was increased by those who came to serve the needs of the monastery.

In 1453, with the Fall of Constantinople, a relatively large number of refugees came to settle on Patmos. They stayed on the west side of the monastery, in the neighborhood that today is called Alloteina, and had an influence on the culture of the island as they introduced a new way of life, and new manners and customs. The conquest of Rhodes by the Turks in 1522 brought new refugees to the island and created the Sofouli complex, which had its own fortification system. This was followed by other similar complexes such as Matali (1599), Pangostas (1606), Mousoudakis (1625) and Syfantos (1636).

Throughout this entire period the monastery was the center of life for the settlement as it was for the whole island. Indeed, it served all the social needs of the inhabitants, replacing the market or the square and serving as the focal point for all aspects of the daily life of the islanders such as festivals and ceremonies. In addition it served as a bank, land registry, notary's office and sometimes as a court of law.

A new wave of refugees from Crete arrived on the island in 1669 after the fall of Chandax (the present-day Herakleion) to the Turks. These new inhabitants settled on the east side of the monastery and their importance lies in the fact that they were the first people to create a planned built center, the square of Ayia Levia around which they also resided.

As the years passed the built form of the island developed at a rapid pace. The houses multiplied and new neighborhoods were created, such as "Aporthiana". That was where the ship captains lived, and from on high they could gaze down proudly on the prowess of their ships anchored in the harbor at Skala.

Above: The Town Hall of Chora and the fountain at the Bousoudakis mansion.
Below: A Patmian seaside dwelling in the countryside.

At the beginning of the 19th century the economy and society of the island were flourishing and this led to the adoption of neoclassicism, a style that was taking root in mainland Greece. Even though it was difficult to completely reproduce this style (because of the crowding together of the plots of land in the already existing settlement) quite a number of houses adopted neoclassical elements. The Town Hall of Chora was built according to that style in 1870.

Stone from the two quarries on Chora was the basic building material for the houses. The roof consisted of the so-called fides which were the trunks of a certain kind of cypress tree. Other materials were cane and "astivi", a kind of shrub employed in the covering of flat roofs. In their ovens they baked the ceramic tiles, with which they laid the Patmian ceramic floors.

Above: The Town Hall of Chora and its square.
Below: The Simantiris mansion/museum in Chora.

The Patmian School

The founding of the Patmian School in the heart of the Monastery of St. John the Divine by the deacon Makarios Kaloyeras was the most important event in the island's history in the 18th century. Today the School lies just above the Cave of the Apocalypse.

The School started operations in the buildings of the Monastery of the Apocalypse in 1713 with a few students from Patmos but as its reputation spread the number of students increased, coming not only from Greece but from its colonies abroad as well.

It developed into one of the most renowned schools of Hellenism with outstanding success in the teaching of the Greek language and Orthodox theology. Until 1912 when its operation was halted by the Italians who had occupied the Dodecanese, it was of invaluable service to the subjugated Greek nation. Its enlightened teachers taught Greek letters to its students and they in their turn distinguished themselves wherever Hellenism was to be found, as Orthodox hierarchs, scholars, scientists and most important of all as heralds of an independent Greece. A prominent graduate of the Patmian School was Emmanuel Xanthos, one of the three founders of the Philiki Etaireia (see History, p. 25).

In 1947 the Patmian School resumed operation in new quarters, next to the old ones, as a Seminary School to which students from all over Greece still come today.

High Mass in the vestibule of the holy Monaster . of St. John the Divine at vespers

Easter On Patmos

Easter, the supreme event in Orthodox Christianity, is celebrated with special magnificence on the holy island of Patmos.

The masses of Easter Week are held at the Monastery of St. John the Divine in accordance with the Byzantine tradition, and all inhabitants strictly observe the Easter fast.

The services begin at nine in the evening and last for many hours with the reading of the appropriate and edifying texts.

The "Ceremony of the Basin" is held on Holy Thursday at 11 in the morning, in Xanthos Square. Based on the Byzantine re-enactment of the Holy Passion, it draws people from all over the Dodecanese, the rest of Greece and even from abroad. It had already become an established tradition by the time of the Turkish occupation when the Greek people endeavored to retain their national identity by means of the Orthodox religion and their language.

The entire ceremony, which is also performed in Jerusalem, is faithfully based on the New Testament. It is performed in commemoration of the Lord's washing of his disciples' feet after the Last Supper and during the reading of the relevant extracts from the Gospel, questions and answers are exchanged between the Abbot, playing the part of Christ, and the hieromonks playing the 12 disciples. The role of Judas is played by the youngest monk. They are all dressed in dark red vestments with floral designs and enter the ceremonial space by twos, accompanied by two deacons, carrying burning incense, and take their places.

In the center of the platform there is a large candle burning and next to it a "chernivolesto", a basin for the washing of the disciples' feet. Then, the Abbot withdraws to pray as if going to the Mount of Olives. The students from the Patmian Seminary School sing in chorus and many eminent figures attend.

On Holy Thursday there is the reading of the Gospels, and at the end is the procession of the Cross ("Today is crucified...") which is carried out in absolute silence.

Scene at the Holy Basin.

On Good Friday the Descent from the Cross is performed with particular brilliance at the Monastery of St. John the Divine but it is also performed at the other churches. In the evening there is a procession of the Epitaphios which takes place in the monastery courtyard while the rest of the churches use the surrounding streets. The ceremony connected to the First Resurrection is also very beautiful. There the Abbot, dressed in multi-colored hand-embroidered vestments, scatters rose and laurel petals over the congregation both inside and outside the church.

On the evening of Holy Saturday the ceremony marking the Resurrection begins with the striking of a "polytalentos". Just before midnight the monastery hands out beeswax candles to all those present and thus the fragrance of the pure wax fills the air as the Resurrection Light is shared out. At precisely midnight the words "Christos Anesti" ("Christ is Risen") are heard accompanied by the joyful sound of a large clapper and an iron gong.

It would be a shame for one to leave after "Christos Anesti" because the divine liturgy of the Resurrection in the main church of the Monastery of St. John the Divine is truly unique. The victory celebration in the triumphal resurrection hymns, the reading of the words of the "Descent into Hades", the ceremony of the "Striking of the Door" during the entrance from the church yard and finally the Catechism Sermon of St. John Chrysostom make for an unforgettable experience. The Resurrection meal after midnight is dominated by the presence of traditional food, the "mageiritsa" Easter soup so necessary after the Holy Week fast. The next day there are the love vespers with the reading of the Gospel in many languages and the handing out of red eggs by the Abbot, when all Patmos goes up to the monastery. Thus there is a prevailing atmosphere of joy and merrymaking, in stark contrast to the deep mourning of Holy Week.

On Easter Tuesday an old custom is still carried out at Ayia Levia square in Chora. The Abbot sprinkles the gathered people with holy water and afterwards the faithful pay their respects to the holy relics that the hieromonks, dressed in gold-embroidered vestments, have brought out as well as the holy icons, which have been carried down from the monastery and the island parishes. Afterward there is a litany in Chora and the procession finishes at the monastery where the divine service ends. Formerly the Abbot would go into the fields and sprinkle holy water on the crops to insure fruitfulness. This is still done at the monasteries of Mt. Athos and at Karyes on Easter Monday when the miracle-working icons are carried in procession.

After the ceremony on Patmos, the clerics take the holy icons around to bless the households, parish by parish, for a new and revitalized life. In the afternoon, the Municipality of Patmos holds an Easter meal with wine at the square in Skala and the young men and women of the island, dressed in local costume, dance Patmian and Dodecanese dances.

The Celebration of the 1900 Year Anniversary of the writing of the Book of Revelation

From the 23rd to the 26th of September 1995 the 1900 year anniversary of the writing of the "Book of Revelation" on Patmos was celebrated with great solemnity and magnificence on the holy island. The crowning event of these celebrations was the convocation of the 2nd Congregation of the Heads of the Orthodox Churches under the chairmanship of the Ecumenical Patriarch Bartholomaios. In the framework of the celebration, two other important conferences were also held: a scholarly one on Revelation itself and its importance and another one concerned with the environment. And of course the celebration of the 1900 year anniversary of Revelation was accompanied by many religious, cultural and commemorative events. There were exhibitions of icon painting, an exhibition of paintings by contemporary artists, a theatrical performance and concert with Irini Pappas, events of a religious character which were attended by many of the faithful and officials, among whom were the President of the Republic of Greece and the Prime Minister, Church dignitaries and many hierarchs.

6

THE HOLY APOCALYPSE

The Holy Cave - The Monastery - The Side-chapels - The Message of the Apocalypse to the Modern World

"The Revelation of Jesus Christ, which God gave unto him, to show unto his servants things which must shortly come to pass..." With these words, words simple and divinely-inspired at one and the same time, unaffected words and for that reason so vital, the "Book of Revelation" begins. A prophetic book, the supreme example of eschatalogical philosophy, a book imbued with the word of God himself: *"I, John...was in the isle that is called Patmos, for the word of God and for the testimony of Jesus Christ. I was in the Spirit on the Lord's day, and heard behind me a great voice, as if of a trumpet, Saying... and, What thou seest, write in a book, and send it unto the seven churches..."*

Exiled, and with a deep faith in God and the need for isolation and contemplation, John found unique refuge in a humble cave on desolate Patmos. And here, in this holy cave, he became a witness and participant in the divine revelation of everything that would happen. As he himself said, he was simply the instrument by which God expressed Himself. That is also why the "Book of Revelation" is the only text of the countless works of apocalyptic literature that was made a part of the "Canon" of the New Testament, being the final book of the Bible. A profound work which has influenced art, politics and even the liturgical life of the Church. All those who have tried to explain it have found it hermetically closed, difficult to explain, but always open to new interpretations or conjectures. This work by John is distinguished for its poetic lucidity and, frequently, for its surrealism, which is why it has always attracted poets and writers. For Orthodox theology, however, it constitutes an inspired, sacred text leading to repentance. If we compare it to a musical concert we could say that the same motifs return every so often while the finale is in the hands of God. Today, after the passage of more than nineteen hundred years, the mysterious flame of the Book of Revelation is still enticingly vivid there in the hollow of the rock, in John's head rest, in the austere reading-stand his disciple used and above all in the triple cleft found on the ceiling, a palpable indication of the Holy Trinity. In the Cave of the Apocalypse, of hope and salvation, the divine presence will never be missing.

The Cave of the Apocalypse

Patmos is the island to which John, the beloved disciple of Christ, was exiled and the cave is the place where he wrote the Book of Revelation. It lies about halfway along the road from Skala to Chora. The holy cave is today enclosed by the Monastery of the Apocalypse which was built more or less around it. This cave is where the "dialogue of love" began between Orthodoxy and Roman Catholicism.

As you start your descent to the holy cave, you pass through the inner courtyard and going down a few steps encounter on the right the side-chapel of Ayios Artemios (St. Artemios) which dates from the 18th century. You continue to descend until you reach a platform from where you can make out to your right the dome of the narthex and the vault of the church of Ayia Anna (St. Anna) with the bell-tower on the left.

After going down the remaining steps you arrive at the entrance to the church of Ayia Anna and the holy cave. The inscription that awaits you at the entrance will flood you with awe and deep emotion:

"**As dreadful as this place is it is nevertheless the house of God and this the Gate of Heaven**".

Moving straight ahead you enter the church of Ayia Anna. According to tradition it was built by Hosios Christodoulos in honor of St. Anna, the mother of the Virgin Mary and because his mother was named Anna as well, but also for Anna Dalassini the mother of the emperor Alexis I Comnenus who advised her son to cede Patmos to him (see page 29). To the right of the church stretches out the holy cave in which is situated the church of St. John the Divine.

The entrance to the Monastery of the Apocalypse.

It is incredibly moving to see the ceiling of the cave, so low that you can touch it, and the terrible cleft in the rock, the triple schism — symbol of the Holy Trinity, through which, according to tradition, John heard the voice of God.

"a great voice as a trumpet saying what thou seest write in a book".

The traces of St. John's residence in the cave can be seen in the niche carved in the rock where he rested his head and another niche that he used to help himself up. Right next to these recesses, at the height of a man, yet not made by any human hand, there is a sort of bookstand where, according to tradition, Prochoros, the disciple of John, wrote down everything that his teacher dictated to him.

Above: The side-chapel of Ayia Anna and below: Mass at the Holy Cave of the Divine Apocalypse.

From the Text of the Book of Revelation

Introductory Vision (I, 9-20)

The commandment from Heaven to record the Visions

I John, your brother in Christ, and your fellow communicant and participant in your tribulations and the persecutions against you for your faith in Christ and in his glorious kingdom and with your patience and hope in Jesus Christ, came in exile to this island that is called Patmos, in order to teach the word of God and for the witness I have born to Jesus Christ.

I came here in spiritual exaltation on a Sunday and heard behind me a great and powerful voice like a sounding trumpet which said to me:

"write in a book, what thou seest and send it unto the seven churches which are in Asia; unto Ephesus, and unto Smyrna, and unto Pergamos, and unto Thyatira, and unto Sardis, and unto Philadelphia, and unto Laodicea".

And there I turned to see the person who had just spoken to me. And when I turned to look I saw seven gold lamps which symbolized the unity of the seven mentioned churches in one spiritual body headed by Christ. And in the middle of the seven lamps I saw a glorious face which seemed like a human face and he was clothed in a magnificent garment which reached down to his feet and was girt about his chest with a gold belt. His head and the hairs on it were as white as white wool, as white as snow and he had the appearance of an old man and his eyes were like flames of fire. His feet were like shining brass as if poured and cleansed in a burning furnace and his voice was as powerful as the sound of many waters falling from a great height. And in his right hand he had seven stars and from his mouth came a sharp two-edged sword symbol of the power of his Word and his right judgement and his face was like the shining sun that shone with all its strength.

And when I saw him, I fell at his feet as if dead. And he laid his right hand upon me, saying unto me:

"Be not afraid, I am the first, because I exist from eternity, and the last, because I will always exist and he that lives forever has life from his very self. And I became dead, because I died but behold despite the death of my crucifixion I have lived for all time and have in my hands the keys of Death and Hell over which I have complete dominion. So write down everything you saw and whatever now exists and whatever will happen from now to the end of the world. And now I will reveal to you the secret meaning of the seven stars, which you saw in my right hand and the seven gold lamps. The seven stars are the seven bishops of the seven churches which represent the whole church, and the seven lamps are the seven churches united in my one and indivisible church...".

The "Book of Revelation" by St. John the Divine is the only prophetic book in the New Testament. The name "Apokalypsis" ("Revelation") refers to the revealing to John by God of things that are destined to happen. The writer mentions the place where he had the visions as the island of Patmos to which he had been exiled. The year the book was written is mentioned as 95 A.D., during the reign of the emperor Domitian.

*(From the New Testament,
Free translation by P. Dimitropoulos)*

God the Father. Wall painting of the Apocalypse, Xeropotamou Monastery, Mt. Athos, 1783.

Brief Summary

The "Book of Revelation" begins with a brief prologue which states that it contains the revelations that Jesus Christ made to John and by means of him to all the faithful. Then the writer identifies himself by name, as well as the ones for whom the message is meant, that is, the seven churches of Asia. He also heralds the coming of Jesus Christ to judge all the races of earth. This is followed by seven epistles to these seven churches, some of which praise and others of which censure.

The description of the visions begins in Chapter 4. The prophet sees God (the beginning of everything) and the Lamb (the beginning of salvation). The Lamb opens a book sealed with seven seals which also means the propagation in mankind of eschatological crises and tribulations.

Then follow the tribulations and the calamities which are proclaimed by seven angels with their seven trumpets. The multitude of voices after the trumpeting of the 7th angel proclaim the triumph of God over the impious.

This is followed by mention of the Kingdom of the Antichrist, the dragon who fell from heaven and the monster that emerged from the sea.

Then the third series of tribulations: seven angels receive seven phials full of divine rage which they successively pour on earth. Christ appears, captures the beast and hurls him into the "lake of fire" for a thousand years when the thousand year kingdom of God will rule. After the passage of the thousand years Satan will undertake the war against the saints but will again be thrown into the "lake of fire" where he will be eternally tormented. Then the prophet sees the Lord seated on a throne while all the dead have been resurrected and are standing before the throne to be judged according to their deeds.

Finally, after thanking the Almighty for everything he heard and saw, John advises everyone to read this prophecy and to keep the commandments of the Lord faithfully.

The Meaning
of the Book of Revelation

According to Orthodox theology the "Book of Revelation" by St. John the Divine is the text, par excellence, to lead one to repentance and salvation. This is also the reason it has been included in the New Testament. At the same time it is of multiple interest: with ecological, poetic, literary, political, pictorial and oracular aspects. It is even connected to tourism and has become the object of extensive theological commentary. The **ecological** aspect is represented by the disasters, pollution, and plagues which were described by John and which can bring people to their senses, people who have not repented before this but have continued to take the name of God in vain and to put the blame on the Slaughtered Lamb. Within the framework of the 900 year anniversary of the Monastery of St. John the Divine on Patmos (1990) the first Environmental Conference was conducted under the auspices of the late Patriarch Dimitrios and the chairmanship of the Professor, Academician and Metropolitan of Pergamon. The Ecumenical Patriarchate has set aside 1 September as a day of prayer for the protection of the environment. And indeed each year on that date there is to be a special ceremony at the Patriarchal Church of Ayios Georgios (St. George) at the Phanari in Istanbul. This service was written by the late Hymnwriter of the Great Church of Christ, the monk Gerasimos Mikrayiannnaitis.

Patriarch Bartholomaios has instituted a yearly conference at the theological school of Chalki in which the President of the Global Fund for Nature, Prince Philip of Great Britain, has taken part, as he did at the Kolymbari meeting outside Chania. An environmental conference was also held at the celebration of the 1900 year anniversary of the "Book of Revelation" (1995).The sacred text also has a poetic character, and is even surreal, one might say. It is not in the least fortuitous that two major poets, George Seferis and Odysseas Elytis, were involved with the translation of the "Book of Revelation" into the living modern Greek language. And both were members of the avant garde of modern Greek poetry.

Patmos, the island of the Apocalypse, has also been a source of inspiration for other poets. Theologians, poets and other literary people have attempted translations of the sacred text. The Book of Revelation has had, in general, a great influence on literature. A professor at the University of Athens, G.K. Pournaropoulos published, in 1984, an article entitled "Modern Prophetic Texts" in "Parnassos", the periodical of the Literary Society where he confirms this influence. Writers (such as Umberto Eco) with a multitude of readers and repeated editions of their works in many languages have confirmed the influence of the "Book of Revelation". The Book of Revelation also has a political aspect. The late Professor Vasileios Stoyiannos at the Theological School of the Aristotelian University of Thessaloniki was referring to precisely this aspect in a speech he gave during a commemorative celebration of the Three Hierarchs (30 January 1985) during which he examined the subject "Revelation and Politics". According to Stoyiannis, The "Book of Revelation" is a drama which unfolds in the terrestrial world while its chorales are sung in the heavenly wings of the set the sole intent being solace. There has been enormous pictorial interest inspired by the "Book of Revelation". Miniaturists, painters, sculptors, engravers, mosaic-makers and others have been inspired down through the centuries, both in the East and the West, by this holy text. In England, Spain, Italy, Holland and Germany exceptional works of art illustrate the "Book of Revelation" or receive their impetus from it. Artists such as the renowned Dürer (1498) exercised great influence. In the following century Holbein (1522) also made woodcuts, like Dürer, which furnished the models for the hagiographer of the external wall of the Refectory of the Dionysiou Monastery on Mt. Athos (which was illustrated from 1520 to 1560). It is not the only monastery on Mt. Athos that has wall paintings from the "Book of Revelation".

In a place of penance such as Mt. Athos, the sacred text naturally has had a profound influence. Thus, from the 16th to the 19th century relevant scenes were painted in other monasteries on the Holy Mountain. The phenomenon is not unique. Designs based on the "Book of Revelation" can also be found at other monastic centers in Greece (Meteora, Patmos, Kastoria, Mistra, Crete and Cyprus). They can be found in Sinai, Bulgaria, Russia and elsewhere as well. It is characteristic that the hieromonk Dionysios from Fourna, Agrafon (1670-1744) supplied extensive instructions for the illustration of the chapters of the "Book of Revelation" in Orthodox churches.

There is an obvious influence of the "Book of Revelation" on the Orthodox liturgy. But also on Romiosyni, the life of ordinary Greeks, particularly during the years they were enslaved by the Turks. Even by the time of Byzantium oracular utterances were very widespread, rendering the various texts in a way that would seem to lend authority to emperors, patriarchs and even prophets.

An ecclesiastical character dominates the commentary of Anthimos, Patriarch of Jerusalem (1788-1808, published in Jerusalem in 1856) based on the teachings that lead to the salvation found in the "Book of Revelation". Those who have occupied themselves in more recent times with the sacred text of St. John include not only university professors and clergymen but philologists.

Studies based on the Book of Revelation are booming in America and Europe. Indeed periodicals specialized in the study and the interpretation of the "Book of Revelation" and the New Testament in general are being continually published.

Down through the years Patmos, the island of the Apocalypse, and especially its holy cave, have been visited by travellers from all around the world.

Pictorial compositions from the Book of Revelation, Dionysiou Monastery, Mt. Athos.

7

THE MONASTERY OF ST. JOHN THE DIVINE

Location - Founding - Architecture - The Main Church - The Side-Chapels - The Library - The Archives - The Museum

Upon entering the narrow bay of Skala, the eye is captured and the soul held in thrall. Built on that once nearly inaccessible high point, the Monastery of St. John the Divine dominates the island with its majestic presence. Impregnable behind its towering stone walls, rivalling the charm and the grandeur of the monasteries of Mt. Athos, the Monastery of St. John the Divine is the repository of history and the profound religious feeling of the centuries. Its founding by Hosios Christodoulos the Laternan in 1088 was the second great event, after the Revelation of God to St. John, that would determine the course of the island's fate. It is a monastery with historical and religious importance which established the monastic tradition on Patmos and bolstered its importance as a place of pilgrimage. But it is also a monastery of exceptional artistic and architectural value: behind its fortress-like, medieval facade is a fortified and labyrinthian complex of cells and installations where priceless religious heirlooms are kept. Wall paintings and rare icons, a sacristry, holy vestments, countless items connected to worship and an invaluable collection of manuscripts, old books and documents have found safe refuge in this holy place. In a place where the spirit breathes freely and is refreshed by the limpid, crystal clear spring of pure Orthodoxy.

Today, the monastery is one of the most forward-looking monastic foundations, keeping the memory of Byzantium burning and making full use of its rich tradition. Here one finds an up-to-date Center of Preservation for icons and manuscripts. Here the monastic and liturgical rituals, which have gone into eclipse in other monastic centers, are also retained with exceptional precision.

The monastery has become cenobitic in our time, with the monks of the Patmian Brotherhood sharing daily meals in common. And here, in this holy place, is where the dialogue with the Roman Catholic Church was launched.

Externally it has the look of a medieval castle while internally it is a multi-level building complex with courtyards, galleries and narrow corridors. The arrangement of the buildings is in accordance with the plan of the Byzantine Orthodox monastery (but in a freer form) where all the cells and the rest of the auxiliary spaces are arranged around the main church. The variation observed at the Monastery of St. John the Divine was created because of the uneven ground (the building complex had to be adapted to it) and the rapid and continuous development of the monastery which resulted in the extension of the building at the expense of its courtyards. The **walls** of the monastery enclosure, polygonal in shape, are 15 meters high; the greatest length from north to south is 53 meters while from east to west it is 70 meters.

The **main entrance** to the monastery dominates the north side of its walls. Formerly there was another opening on the south side, but it has now been closed off. The entrance consists of two rectangular towers which are joined to the wall in back. On the top part of the wall there is a small opening from which burning hot oil or water or even lead was once poured on invaders who threatened to violate the gate. Above the lintel, in a semicircular arch, the icon of St. John the Divine remains the unsleeping guard and protector of the monastery. In front of this entrance is the chapel of Ayioi Apostoloi (The Holy Apostles) founded in 1603.

1. Section of the walls of the holy monastery.
2. Interior spaces in the monastery.
3. The bell-tower and machicolations on the monastery.
4. Resting in front of the entrance to the Great Monastery outside the chapel of Ayioi Apostoloi.

3

4

The **courtyard** in the center of the monastery is laid with pebbles and decorated with arches. On its north and west sides can be seen the white walls of the cells. On the south side of the courtyard is the "Tzafara", a two-storey arched gallery built in 1698. A more recent gallery with four arches is situated in front of the outer galille of the main church on the east side. The inscriptions found left of the entrance to the courtyard indicate the placement of the tombs of Grigorios, the Metropolitan of Didymoteichos (1963) and Neophytos, the Patmian Ecumenical Patriarch (1747). In the monastery enclosure are the chapels of Ayioi Pantes (All Saints), Stavros (Holy Cross), Ayios Vasileios (St. Basil), Ayios Nikolaos (St. Nikolas) and Ayios Ioannis Vaptistis (St. John the Baptist).

1. View of the monastery's inner courtyard.

2. The sheltered spaces and the monastery bell-towers.

3. The fortress-like enclosure (courtyard) of the monastery.

1

2

The **main church** of the **monastery** was one of the first buildings to be created, as it was completed around 1090. The carved wooden iconostasis of the main church, the hanging silver lamps and the priceless chandeliers create a pious atmosphere which is supplemented by the Byzantine psalmody. Here the monastic conventions and, of course, the traditions of the monastery are observed as nowhere else. The more elderly monks keep vigilant watch on the younger ones to make sure they do not change, do not eliminate or corrupt anything. Even today one can hear at the Monastery of St. John the Divine the slow tempo of the Byzantine hymn, "Joyous Light". The main church is an inscribed cruciform church with four columns, to which were later added the gallery on the facade and the side-chapels. The floor of the church consists of marble slabs. The carved wooden iconostasis is more recent, dating from 1820, and was the gift of Nektarios, the Patmian metropolitan of Sardis. This iconostasis replaced an older one (from the 15th century) which in its turn had replaced the original stone iconostasis which Hosios Christodoulos had placed there.
The church was built on the ruins of an Early Christian basilica, while in antiquity there was a temple to Artemis on the same site.
The large icon of the Apocalypse on the north wall of the church is a gift of Nikiphoros, the Bishop of Laodicia. This icon covers the entrance to the new sacristry also built by Nikiphoros to house his books. Today valuable heirlooms are kept there.

Above: In the outer galilee just before the start of Vespers.
Below: The striking of the wooden simantron at predetermined moments of the Holy Mass.

The famed carved wooden iconostasis of the main church a gift of the Patmian Metropolitan of Sardis, Nektarios (1820).

The **old sacristy** is on the left side of the main church (it is not open to visitors). Here are kept sacredotal vessels, marvelous icons done by Cretan hagiographers, vestments and sacred relics as well as the miracle-working holy skull of the Apostle Thomas. It also contains the Gold Bull of Alexis I Comnenus by which the emperor ceded Patmos to Hosios Christodoulos.

On the right side of the main church, in the south section of the inner galilee, is a door leading to the side-chapel of Hosios Christodoulos. It is dated to the 17th century and, at his own behest, the venerable relics of the Blessed Christodoulos were deposited there, placed within a gold and silver sarcophagus.

The silvered sarcophagus containing the venerable skull of Hosios Christodoulos.

Detail from the sarcophagus of Hosios Christodoulos.

The side-chapel of the Panayia (The Virgin Mary) is on the south side of the church and was built in the 12th century A.D. It is of small dimensions (8.40x3.05 m.) and is covered by a barrel vault. Its floor is made of marble and its carved wooden iconostasis is dated to 1607, when it replaced the older marble one. The side chapel is illustrated with Byzantine wall paintings of unsurpassed artistry. The exit from the side-chapel of the Panayia gives onto a staircase leading to the secretary's office, the Abbot's quarters and the Synod. Photographs of former abbots, of ceremonial basins and of the Brotherhood decorate the walls. The Synod is where coffee is offered on feast days and official occasions, and is accompanied by the renowned Patmian pastries, the so-called "pogia", which are filled with almonds and honey.

Behind the main church is the **old refectory** of the monastery with the remains of wall paintings. The refectory was the place where the monks formerly dined. Its construction was completed by 1090 and so this too was one of the first buildings in the monastery. The room is nearly square (6.32x6.60 m.) and is 8.50 m. high. In the center and running along the room are two tables dressed with marble, and separated by an aisle.

Along the sides of the tables are grooves in which the monks placed their personal articles of food. Here is where the official meal was served during the visit of the Ecumenical Patriarch Bartholomaios in 1994.

On the south side of the refectory was the kitchen and next to it the milling room. The **new refectory** is on the other side of the monastery and one reaches it by turning right on leaving the courtyard. The monastery also had a storeroom for supplies (below the south gallery of the courtyard) and next to it a storeroom for olive oil, a bread-baking room, a bread-kneading room and "kisternes" (cisterns) for the water supply.

Above: St. John of Damascus and St. Kosmas Melodos. A wall painting in the Panayia side-chapel.

Below: The low relief carved wooden iconostasis of the side-chapel of the Panayia, 1607.

The **peristyle library** of the monastery was also founded by Hosios Christodoulos who brought his valuable collection of books with him who when he emigrated to Patmos. Since that time a large number of donors have enriched it with so much material it is now considered one of the most important and libraries in the East. Its books are divided into the old ones, which are found together with the manuscripts in the main room, and the more modern. It operates according to the most up-to-date technical standards of library science serving an enormous number of visitors as well as researchers and other interested parties throughout the world to whom are sent microfilms of the library's works. The library is famous for its Byzantine and post-Byzantine manuscripts, its old publications, its extremely valuable document archives and its contemporary bibliography. It has developed into an international center of Byzantine and post-Byzantine studies where scholarly work can be pursued to its full potential.

The monastery's peristyle library.

Above the library is the new sacristy and museum in which are sensitively displayed icons of various periods, mainly Byzantine, and other heirlooms. Here are the relics of saints which have been placed in extremely valuable and artistically ornamented reliquaries, vestments made of rare and precious fabrics and embroidered with gold or silver and mitres of emperors and patriarchs made of gold and precious stones. In addition, one finds Patmian furniture, objects of silver and gold, and gold and lead bulls from the treasures of the monastery. Today there are two very important centers operating in the museum for the preservation of icons and documents and equipped with the most up-to-he-minute instruments.

The archives of the monastery contain about 13,000 documents, the oldest of which dates from 1073, representing the entire history of the monastery. One of the first documents of this collection was the gold bull which founded the monastery and its accompanying documentation. There are also other bulls (documents written on parchment and signed by the emperor of Byzantium), the papers, codicil and secret testament of Hosios Christodoulos as well as Latin, Turkish and Rumanian documents.

1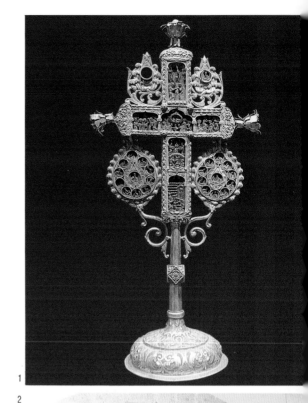

2

1. The fabulous carved wooden cross (used for blessing) made of silver and bordered by dozens of iconographic compositions.

2. Space for the hanging and exhibition of the gold bulls in the monastery.

3., 4. Views of the holy monastery from the museum.

3

4

STROLLING THROUGH CHORA

Churches - Architecture - Squares - Lanes

Commanding, imperious and dynamic, the Monastery of St. John the Divine has been standing vigilantly at the top of the hill for centuries now trumpeting the Orthodox Christian faith and the peaceful life of its residents. And when you stand on its lofty stone walls with their lacy ramparts and the historic machicolations and gaze up at the far distant horizon and the infinity of the sea you feel you are but a step from the throne of God on High. Up here the eye is liberated and embraces the blue magic of the sea with its lovely beaches and the steely beauty of the sheer coastal cliffs, elements which are part and parcel of the island's mysterious character. Beneath the enormous walls of this watchful guard and beacon of Orthodoxy and the Greek tradition, lies Chora, set in an imposing and dazzling white circle, and bathed in Aegean light. Grand two and three-storey mansions, with carved wooden ceilings and old lamps with polychrome opal shades, picturesque traditional houses with open areas and blooming gardens, along with all the many flagged lanes and small squares, lure the visitor into unforgettable labyrinthian streets. The courtyards of the houses are internal ones. Inscriptions and carvings, crosses and dates can be observed here and there on the lintels over the entrances, on the facades of the churches or the metopes of the small, quaint bell-towers. The vaults, the so-called katounia, with their flag-stone lanes, create charming galleries containing various sized open areas which are reminiscent of bygone eras. The large courtyards and handful of wooden balconies are covered with all kinds of flowers and smell sweetly all the seasons of the year. There's a little church at every turn, every glance reminds one of the great faith that has ruled this island for centuries. The pure white traditional houses in one large and tight embrace, picturesque tavernas here and there, and grocer's shops and squares such as Ayia Levia and Emmanuel Xanthos, transport you to the land of dreams.

1

2

4

Going up the old flagstoned road from Skala, you slowly enter the special atmosphere that dominates Chora, the heart of Patmos. This is where the holy history of the island, still so vital, declares its living presence through a host of exceptional churches: Megali Panayia (The Great Virgin), Ayios Vasileios (St. Basil), Ayios Nikolaos (St. Nikolas), Ayios Ioannis Prodromos (St. John the Forerunner), Panayia ton Koimitirion (Our Lady of Eternal Rest), the Ypapanti (The Presentation) and of course Panayia Diasozousa (Our Lady of Rescue) which dates to 1599. This church has achieved great fame due to its icon of "Ayia Diasozousa" or "Ayia Sozousa", the venerable icon of the Virgin Mary well-known to all the faithful for its miracles.

1. Old windmills, the living reminders of the past.

2. The flagstoned lanes of Chora create a special atmosphere.

3. The Panayia Diasozousa in Chora.

4. The miracle-working icon of the Panayia Diasozousa.

Chora is connected to the harbor at Skala and the other settlements on the island by an asphalt road. There is also an old stone-paved road which is used for the ascent with pack animals and today makes for a pleasant stroll for the visitor who wants to experience the special atmosphere of this holy island.

Above: Passing by the mansions in Chora.

Below: donkeys ready to haul goods.

On opposite page: Partial view of Chora.

Outside its churches, the architecture of Chora is also of interest, both for the external formation of its spaces and the internal arrangement of the houses. A prime example of a traditional Patmian house is the Simantiris mansion, next to the monastery of Zoodochos Pigi, which has opened wide its doors to the visitor. This is a house/monument, built in 1625 by master craftsmen from Smyrna, but also a house/museum, which is full of priceless objects from the past: furniture up to 250 years old, unique paintings, an iconostasis with paintings done in the Russian technique from the 14th, 15th and 16th century. Just one site of the hundreds in Chora, but which cannot be definitely listed because the list would vary according to personal taste. The feeling is of another time, one of purity and faith.

Below: Skala as seen from Chora.

On opposite page: From the interior of the Simantiris mansion.

9

MONASTERIES & HERMITAGES

The Convent of Evangelismos - The Convent of Zoodochos Pigi - The Convent of Ayia Ayion - The Hermitages

Patmos, symbol of faith and communication with God, is still today a pole of attraction for monks from all over the world. This humble "Sinai of the Aegean", by now a traditional place for asceticism and prayer, has opened its embrace to many monasteries, kathismata (small monastic units) and hermitages. There are a considerable number of kathismata and hermitages on Patmos. These are tranquil and isolated locations containing a chapel with small cells where one or more monks live a religious and moral life according to their own precepts. Orthodox monasticism was created by the purely spiritual quest of the monks and by an inner desire to go to isolated locations to forge their faith and hammer out their personality by ceaselessly worshipping their Creator. In the kathismata and hermitages the monks live as ascetics working and worshipping God with fasts, all night vigils and a great deal of prayer. Behind the severity of the canons that they so faithfully apply, there is also the tradition of the Greek soul which is distinguished for its hospitality, its sense of sacrifice and its tireless endeavor for spiritual elevation. The endless prayers of the monks are not simply for their own salvation but the salvation of the entire world. They do not only look to their own inner visions and listen to their own inner cries, but to the cries of a desire for personal negation and repentance, a repentance for all the world and all the nations, "those that are lawless and those that observe the law". At the same time they themselves through their ceaseless prayers and the constancy of their liturgical, mysterious life, are lifted beyond the "built" world, giving up all contact with manufactured things and come into union with the divine.

For each ascetic, in line with the measure of his own personal elevation, dissolves the darkness of death, the fear of judgement, the abyss of Hell and directs his eyes to the "Lord arriving in Glory".

The Convent of Evangelismos

The Convent of Evangelismos Mitros Egapimenou (The Annunciation to the Mother of the Beloved One) is located at the monastic dependency of the Evangelistria (Our Lady of the Annunciation) on the southwest side of Chora on a very lovely bay. The dependency was built in 1613 by a hieromonk from the Monastery of St. John the Divine, Nikiphoros Kretas, who was from Crete. It is built on the side of a deep ravine, like a platform. The rock which soars up round it has its roots fed by the rushing stream of Keras Leousa ending at the "Gardens of Hosios" on the bay of the same name on the west coast of Patmos, facing the Icarian sea.

The dependency consists of the church of the Evangelistria, the side-chapel of Ayios Loukas (St. Luke) and a three-storey defensive tower with the side-chapel of Ayios Antonios (St. Anthony).

Views of the Convent of Evangelismos Mitros Egapimenou.

As the inscription on the inner lintel of Ayios Loukas states, Nikiphoros built it out of gratitude to the saint. During his residence at the hermitage he was attacked by the deadly disease of plague; he prayed to the Evangelist Luke who cured him.

The founding of the Convent of the Evangelismos dates to 1937 and was the work of the hieromonk from the Monastery of St. John the Divine, Amphilochos Makris. This old man was a great spiritual figure and worked hard for the establishment and the development of the convent. Both the dependency of the Evangelistria and the Convent of Evangelismos Mitros Egapimenou carried on noteworthy activity during a difficult period for the Greek nation. During the Occupation in the Dodecanese, when the Italians forbade the use of the Greek language, a "secret school" was organized there where nuns, who were teachers, taught. After the liberation of the Dodecanese, Amphilochos Makris was asked to send a group of nuns to help organize the orphanage on Rhodes.

This mission was indeed carried out and the group of nuns set up at one and the same time a foudling hospital, a nursery school and a public school. Besides the orphanage on Rhodes the nuns are today occupied with beekeeping, vegetable gardening, flower gardening, icon painting and the sewing of religious garments and embroidery. In embroidery the "spitha" ("sword") stitch was traditionally connected to Patmos. Its teaching goes all the way back to the time of Hosios Christodoulos when this stitch was used on the embroideries of the aristocratic families of Byzantium.

But with the passage of time it was forgotten until Amphilochos Makris himself urged the nuns to revive it.

The icon painter, Sister Olmypiada, a student of Fotis Kontoglou, the great Byzantine icon painter, belongs to the holy sisterhood of the convent.

The Convent of Zoodochos Pigi

The Convent of Zoodochos Pigi ("Life-Giving Source") lies to the southwest of the Holy Monastery of St. John the Divine and is the second most populous convent on the island, after Evangelismos. It was founded in 1607 by the Patmian hieromonk Parthenios Pangostas. Its nuns carry out laudable philanthropic work while at the same time occupying themselves with handicrafts: embroidery, the sewing of religious garments and so on.

Ecclesiastical traditions are carried on here as well, including the ceremonies for the feast-day of the Virgin Mary, on 15 August, consisting of the minor and major Paracletian Canon and the funeral, with the eulogies for the Virgin, just like the eulogies delivered on Good Friday.

The Convent of Ayia Ayion

In Chora, and near the Convent of Zoodochos Pigi, is the small convent of Ayia Ayion (Holy Saints).

Above: A pebbled courtyard full of flowers from the Convent of Zoodochos Pigi.

Below: Interior view from the Convent of Ayia Ayion.

The Hermitages of Patmos

The holy island of Patmos has been a pole of attraction for hermits, ascetics and monks, who feel a profound need for peace and quiet, for contemplation and prayer to God. During the period of the Turkish occupation the "kollyvades" (a group of religious traditionalists) came to the island from Mt. Athos and founded a host of hermitages and monastic dependencies which preserved the traditions of the island's spiritual relationships to that revivalist movement on Athos. The Patmians take care of the hermitages and hold feasts at them when the little church at a given hermitage celebrates the memory of the saint in whose honor it was built.

The Holy Kathisma of Profitis Ilias Thesvitos

This lies southwest of Chora on top of the highest peak on the island (260 m.). The view from the church is incredible. The whole island is spread out at one's feet; the hills, the small plains, the lacy coastline and the settlements. This kathisma was built in 1764 by the hieromonk Neophytos of Simi. The building complex consists of a small fortress with the church of Profitis Ilias (Prophet Elijah) in the center. The church is single-aisled with a dome and celebrates on 20 July. The view from there is unique and rewards the visitor.

The kathisma of Profitis Ilias.

The Kathisma of Panayia Grava. This lies between Kalamoti hill and the Evangelismos convent west of Chora. It was built around 1775 by Grigorios of Nisyros, the hieromonk Niphonas and other monks who fleeing Mt. Athos ended up on Patmos. The small church is dedicated to the Koimisis tis Theotokou (The Dormition of the Virgin) and celebrates on the name day of the Virgin Mary (15 August). Its founder is thought to have been the hieromonk Grigorios Gravanos of Nisyros.

The Hermitage of Petra. This lies south of Groikos on the Kallikatzous rock. The rock was used as a hermitage during the time of Hosios Christodoulos.

The Kathisma of Hosios Christodoulos. In the area of Alykes there is a small church dedicated to Hosios Christodoulos whose iconosta-sis has a miracle-working icon which depicts Hosios Christodoulos offering the monastery to St. John.

The Hermitage of Panayia Epsimia. As you pass through Groikos, you see a dirt road to the right which leads to the hermitage. It consists of a small church dedicated to the Panayia tou Stavrou (Our Lady of the Cross) and cells. Hosios Christodoulos is mentioned as its founder. It is named Epsimia ("Ripener") because September, when the church celebrates, is the month when the late crops (the "opsimo") ripen; in the local dialect this is "epsimia".

The Bapistry. The area of Sykamia is on the road leading from Chora to Groikos. There is found the cave in which St. John the Divine baptized people and made them Christians. One can still see the clay pipes which were used to transport the water from the spring to the "Bapistry". Archaeologists believe it to be a section of an Early Christian basilica, ruins of which have been located in the area.

The Cave of Kynopas. On the southwest end of the island lies the cave of Kynopas or Genoupas, near the cape of the same name, on the slopes of a hill, also with the same name. According to tradition, Kynopas was a pagan magician, and was opposed to St. John the Divine preaching the Gospel. Today there is a chapel there to Ai-Yannis tou Spilioti (St. John the "Cave-Dweller") that celebrates on 8 May.

The Kouvari Hermitage. This lies on the northern shores of the bay of Stavros. Its proprietor was the hieromonk Amphilochos Makris, the later founder of the Convent of Evangelismos Mitros Egapimenou. He also founded a monastic dependency for men, dedicated to Iosif Mnistora (Joseph the Bethrothed).

The Kathisma of Ayia Paraskevi of Kavos. This lies to the left of the "Gardens of Hosios" on the southwest side of the island. It consists of cells and the small church of Ayia Paraskevi which has a miracle-working icon; it celebrates on 26 July.

The hermitage of Petra.

The Kathisma of Panayia Koumanas.

On the north side of the bay of Skala can be seen Mt. Koumana.
The name is probably derived from the former renter of the area, Koumanis, a name already known by the 13th century. On the ridge of this steep mountain is the kathisma of Ayioi Pantes (All Saints) or the Panayia tis Koumanas as the locals call it in honor of the miracle-working icon found there. Its proprietor was Ayios Makarios Notaras the Corinthian.

Above: The iconostasis of the kathisma's church.
Below: The building complex of the Panayia Koumana.

The Kathisma of Apollos. *This lies northeast of Yeranos in the area of Thermia, and is named after the one who founded it, a certain Apollos. It consists of a small church, cells and a walled-in enclosure. This church has a tale surrounding it's erection: during one of the all night vigils which took place in the Monastery of St. John the Divine, Apollos delivered the reading connected to the particular feast-day. There was a ship-master there, Captain Lazaris, who had been forced by bad weather to stay on the island. He was so impressed by this reading that he inquired about Apollos, learned all about him and visited him at his hermitage to ask him if he needed anything. Apollos replied that he needed nothing. But in the end he revealed that he had the desire to found a small church and the captain hastened to satisfy this desire, selling the rice that he had in the hold of his ship and giving the money to Apollos. The church that was founded was dedicated to Ayioi Pantes (All Saints).*

The Leivadi ton Kaloyeroi *(The "Monks' Meadow"). This lies on the north side of the island, south of Cape Sardella.*
It was called the "Meadow of Koutroulis", after the name of its original proprietor.
In the 18th century the hieromonk Parthenios Partheniades, one of the Kollyvades, arrived on Patmos, accompanied by several other monks and the Meadow of Koutroulis was ceded to him by its owners on the condition that he pay them 25 piastres a year.
Thus he became the first proprietor of the dependency and for that reason it is called the kathisma of Parthenios.

On opposite page: The kathisma of Apollos at the little harbor bubbling from the hot springs.

Below: The Livadi ton Kaloyeron and monastery (Kathisma Parthenis).

10

THE HARBOR

After many hours of meandering through the blue waters of the Aegean the ship at last arrives at its destination: the harbor of Skala. Each day cruise ships bring visitors who are in a hurry. The buses await them to take them up to Chora to see the famous monastery. Chora is the largest settlement on the island today, the commercial, economic and social center of its life, as well as the settlement with the most rapid development.

At the beginning of the 17th century there were only a few warehouses in Skala and some installations for the servicing of boats.

The inhabitants of that time, fearing pirate raids, found security in the embrace of Chora, beneath the mighty fortress-like Monastery of St. John the Divine.

But with the passage of time conditions changed and by the 19th century the inhabitants began to gradually come down to Skala and to transform it into a commercial and shipping center. The crowning point of this development took place after the liberation of the island from the Italians and its union with the rest of Greece. Its true development started then with new enterprises and hotels, commercial shops and restaurants, but it has been a discreet development that has preserved the picturesque element of the place.

The top of the hill above the harbor of Skala is commanded by the imposing Monastery of St. John the Divine.

OF SKALA   the center of the island

A multitude of little houses that spread out and
ascend the slopes of the surrounding heights
fill this settlement with abundant island color,
and lifting one's eyes even higher there is
Koumana, the mountain that plays host to the
more "famous" kathismata on the island.
Today in Skala the visitor can admire the local
traditional architecture, and the beautiful
beaches, and have a good time in the
tavernas, or the night-clubs with folk music as
well as watch Greek and foreign films at the
cinemas and afterward enjoy the exceptional
local pastries.

1. Aerial photograph of Skala.
2. The picturesque little harbors of Skala, Merikas and
Chochlakas.
3. Skala from the chapel of Ayia Paraskevi.
4. Skala on a summer afternoon.

On Easter Sunday dignitaries, locals and foreign visitors pass by the police station to offer best wishes and to taste the lamb roasted on a spit, even though the traditional custom of the Patmians was to roast stuffed lamb in the oven. In the afternoon of the same day all the inhabitants of the island go up to the great Monastery of St. John the Divine to receive the blessing of the abbot and some tsoureki (brioche) and red eggs. And then on the afternoon of Easter Monday the municipality holds a fabulous celebration offering roast lamb, tasty baked stuffing and wine to young and old, foreigners and locals, while young men and women, in traditional local costumes dance island dances to the accompaniment of musical instruments.

1. *The little harbor of Ayia Paraskevi with fishing boats and fishermen.*
2. *Skala, the picturesque little harbor.*
3. *Headquarters.*
4. *The harbor of Skala at dusk.*

3

4

If you happen to enter the harbor of Skala in the evening, a large illuminated cross on the top of the hill to the right will prepare you for the fact that you are visiting a holy island. After but a taste of the deep religiosity and the history of the island, the visitor to Skala is then free to choose his own personal course on Patmos either by taxi, rented car, motorbike or bus to Chora, Groikos and Kambos or by small craft to Lambi and Psili Ammo and Leipsoi using Skala as a base of operations for his wanderings.

Above: The Bapistry of St. John the Divine (ruined building) 96 A.D.
Below: Skala, area of Ayia Paraskevi.

On opposite page: Skala, the holy church of Ayios Phocas.

11

COUNTRYSIDE & BEACHES

North of Skala - South of Skala

Dotted with small settlements, bays and beaches, Patmos holds continual surprises in store for the visitor. An island endowed with both a mysterious atmosphere and a lovely nature, it reveals a complex character which is sure to charm everyone.

With your base of operations the harbor of Skala, the center of tourism and vitality, and heading to the north of the island you will reach a series of hospitable beaches.

There are the beaches of Merikas in the bay of the same name, Meloi with dense vegetation and Agriolivado with its calm waters and lovely view of the islet of Ayia Thekla opposite. The picturesque settlement of Epano Kambos is further north, with its traditional dances and festivals held on the celebration of the Dormition of the Virgin Mary. The beach connected to the settlement, Kato Kambos, is a focus of all the social activity on the island. In its blue waters you can enjoy your favorite sea sport and along the shore small tavernas have authentic, tasty local dishes for your delectation. If you like deserted beaches, North Patmos has a lot to offer you: the path to pebbled Vayia, and

Linginos and Leivadi that goes down to the bay of Yeranos. Do not omit a visit to Lambi with its marvelous colored pebbles, unique in the world, which gleam with their own natural briliance under the light of the summer sun. The north also has another beach, truly enchanting, called Lefkes, which is near Kambos. There the wild and lonely landscape is completely in harmony with the old, abandoned tower, giving one a strong feeling of isolation and tranquillity.

But the south side of Patmos is not lacking in beauty either. The beach at Groikos has a good reputation, is well suited to tourists, and is able to provide a comfortable stay for any visitor. A pleasant walk to the south over a narrow band of earth will lead you to the rock of Kallikatzous where the rare birds of the region nest. This rock, has wells hollowed out in it and its paths have inspired many legends. It is said that the hermitage of Hosios Christodoulos was here.

Psili Ammos, even further south, is a large quiet beach with golden sand and is considered to be one of the most beautiful on the island. It is well worth a visit.

North of Skala
Netia - Merikas - Meloi

*Setting off from **Skala** and heading north, you reach the nearest coastal settlement at **Netia**. Left from the crossroads that leads to Netia is a dirt road that goes to the beautiful beach of **Merikas**. From there the first turn-off takes you to the back part of the elevation of **Koumana** while the other ends at the bay of **Aspri** where in 1973 traces were found of a Bronze Age settlement. Right of Netia, the road leads to the bay of Meloi. The beach, which also has a camping site, is a lovely nearby refuge.*

Below: Merikas.
On opposite page: Views from Meloi.

Agriolivado - Ayia Thekla

*Continuing along the main road, a turn-off right leads to the quiet bay of **Agriolivado**. It is 35 minutes from Skala on foot. The view of the island opposite, **Ayia Thekla**, helps complete its beautiful image.*

Lefkes

Lefkes, with a beach of the same name, has a special, enchanting beauty. You can reach it by turning left at the intersection of the main road which goes from Skala to Kambos. The wild landscape is perfect for all those seeking isolation and tranquillity.

Above: The islet of Ayia Thekla opposite the bay of Agriolivado.

Below: The picturesque and beautiful harbor of Agriolivado.

Epano Kambos

The main road north takes you to the picturesque settlement of **Epano Kambos**. It is the island's third most populous settlement and since 1937 its square has been dominated by the church of the Evangelismos. Each year on 25 March (the day the Annunciation is celebrated) and 14 August (the eve of the feast day of the Dormition of the Virgin) there is a large celebration there with local dances and music.

1. The church of the Evangelismos tis Theotokou.
2.,3.,4., Scenes and images from Epano Kambos.
5. The picturesque harbor of Kato Kambos.

1
3

2

4

5

Kato Kambos

If you stay on the road which passes through the settlement, you will descend to the beach, to **Kato Kambos**, the best known and most socially active beach on the island. The calm waters of its bay are suitable, on the one hand, for endless hours of swimming and games and on the other for the enjoyment of various kinds of sea sports (it is possible to rent equipment there). And there are always tavernas around ready to offer you delicious tidbits.

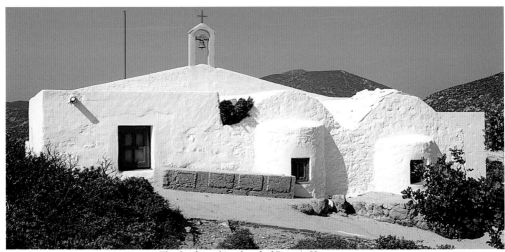

The dazzling white chapel of Panayia Yeranos.

Vayia - Linginos - Bay of Yeranos

A ten minute hike from the beach of Kambos takes you to the bay of **Vayia**. Few people go there, the water is invigoratingly clean and the smattering of trees provide its pebbled beach with shade. Those who are not averse to walking can also visit the beach of **Linginos** at **Leivadi,** ending at the bay of **Yeranos**. The whole route from Vayia to Yeranos takes about 40 minutes on foot but it can be shortened if you follow the asphalt road which starts at Kambos.

The Leivadi of Yeranos.

Kentronisi - Ayios Georgios

On the SW side of Cape Yeranos is Kentronisi. Next to **Kentronisi** is the small islet of **Ayios Georgios** with its chapel of the same name (St. George).

On opposite page: The lacy coastline and picturesque islets in the area of Linginos and Yeranos.

The Kathisma of Apollos

Along the route going toward the hill of Yeranos you will see on your left, to the north, the picturesque **kathisma of Apollos**. On Yeranos hill there is a small church dedicated to the Panayia (Virgin Mary) and there is also an enchanting view from there toward the lacey shores to the west.

Leivadi ton Kaloyeron

Going toward the beach at Lambi there is a dirt road to the west which leads after a half an hour's walk to **Leivadi ton Kaloyeron**. This wide plain next to the sea is planted with garden vegetables. It is a site of unique natural beauty and harmony. The small chapel there has been built in the Byzantine style and is dedicated to the Dormition of the Virgin Mary.

Above: the kathisma of Apollos and below: the Livadi ton Kaloyeron, in a Paradise-like setting.

Lambi

The beach at Lambi lies on the north side of the island and one can get there by turning left at the junction with the asphalt road after the beach of Kambos. One can also go there by caique from Skala (the trip takes about 1 hour). Its multicolored and unusual pebbles are a pole of attraction for a large number of its visitors who do not go there just to swim in its sparkling clean water, but also to gather up the pebbles and to create their own original collection of them. Indeed, this beach could be called nothing else but Lambi ("Shining"), as the shining of the sun on the sea and the multicolored pebbles is bewitching. In the same region you can also make out the ruins of an ancient settlement which was called Platys Yialos.

The small harbor of Lambi and the beach with the colored pebbles.

Left of the road which leads to Lambi and behind a rocky height is the church of the Metamorphosis tou Sotiros (The Transfiguration) from the 16th century. Each year, on 5 August (its feast day) the holy liturgy is performed by the abbot of the Monastery of St. John the Divine followed by a celebration at the tavernas of Kambos. There is also a church there dedicated to the Panayia Parthena (The All Holy Virgin) which celebrates on 23 August.

Ayios Nikolaos Avdelas

West of Lambi a road leads to **Ayios Nikolaos** ton **Evdilos** or **Avdelas**. In that place lived many of the families of the artisans and master craftsmen that Hosios Christodoulos brought to Patmos to erect the Monastery of St. John the Divine.

The chapel of St. John Avdelas which is considered to be one of the oldest churches on Patmos (11th century).

Colored pebbles on the beach at Lambi.

The secure bay of St. John Evdilos or Avdelas where caiques and other craft anchor.

South of Skala

Groikos

Following the paved coastal road south of Skala you arrive at one of the island's best known beaches, Groikos. You can also get there on the main road that passes through Chora.

Kallikatzous rock

Heading south along a dirt road you reach a narrow sandy strip of land which ends at **Kallikatzous** rock where the Petra hermitage is (see page 86). The rock is 10 m. high and has a circumference of 80 m. It got its name from the birds that roost there, known as "kallikatzoudes".

1. View of Groikos.
2. Skala, your starting point for south Patmos.
3. Aerial photograph of Groikos with the Kallikatzous rock.

1

Its impressive outline, the carved recesses and the carved steps that lead to its top have inspired the inhabitants of the island to create a number of legends connected to it. But it is a fact that this sheer rock was used as a hermitage during the time of Hosios Christodoulos. Today traces are still found, most probably left by ascetics, as one can make out carved places used for shelves, the opening of an oven, a well and a pipeline for the transport of water.

At the base of the rock, on its SE side and in the sea, can be seen the foundations of the church of the Panayia Fylachtomeni or Fylassousi (Our Lady the "Guardian") and a column which is thought to have been the base of an altar.

Tragonisi

This small, uninhabited island lies opposite the Kallikatzous rock.

Diakofti - Stavros - Psili Ammos

South of the bay of Petra is Diakofti, the narrowest point on the island. It is 200 meters wide and on its west side is the beautiful sand beach of **Stavros.** Right next to it, to the south, is **Psili Ammos,** a quiet, large beach, one of the most beautiful on the island. You feel like you are in the desert walking along its fine golden sand. A caique, leaving from the harbor of Skala, is the only way to get there.

Alykes

Alykes lies on the north end of Stavros bay. This area is where the monks collect salt and the one responsible for this work is called "alykaris" (from "alyki" which means "salty" in Greek). The kathisma of Hosios Christodoulos is also to be found there.

The enchanting beach at Groikos. On opposite page: Diakoftis and Alykes (aerial photograph).

12

THE NEARBY SMALL ISLANDS

Petrokaravo - Leipsoi - Arkoi - Agathonisi
Practical Informations

Patmos is surrounded by many small islands, like satellites, and one could say that this part of the Aegean archipelago has a "polynesian" character ("polynisia" = many islands). Some of these islands have a number of inhabitants and others not so many, but all are worth visiting either on one of the scheduled boats or by renting one of your own; these settlements are small paradises and nature there retains something of the original Creation. The water is clear and crystalline. The sand beaches are lovely and as clean as the water. Some of them have installations that are suitable for more than one day's stay. There are also uninhabited islands around Patmos, some of which you may have seen on your tour of the island, such as the picturesque Ayia Thekla, in the bay of

Agriolivado, Ayios Georgios and Kentronisi off Cape Yeranos and Tragonisi off the coast of Groikos opposite the Kallikatzous Rock. These small islands help complete the blue and white mosaic of Patmos.

Anydros - Petrokaravo

NW of the Leivadi ton Kaloyeron is the small island of Anydros and SW Petrokaravo behind which can be seen Icaria. Seen from one side Petrokaravo looks like a boat ("Petrokaravo" = "stone boat"). According to tradition this was a pirate ship with 40 pirates that was headed toward the island to plunder it. The guardian of the island, Hosios Christodoulos, turned it to stone by fervent prayer and along with it its life preservers which are now very small little islets scattered all around it.

Leipsoi

This little island lies 11 km. east of Patmos and has connections with the harbor of Skala. It has an area of 16 square kilometers and its inhabitants, numbering approximately 600, are involved for the most part with cultivating the land and fishing. The highest mountain, in the eastern part of the island, is no more than 300 meters high. There are beautiful bays all around and in one of them, the largest and most enclosed, is the harbor and only settlement on Leipsoi. The island is dotted with hermitages and kathismata, the best known being the Panayia tou Charou (Our Lady of Death) which dates to 1600. It is called that because the icon found there depicts the Virgin Mary holding her Crucified Son and not the more usual infant. This icon has another feature: each year, on the Virgin Mary's feast-day the lilies hung on it, all dried up since the feast-day of the Annunciation (25 March) suddenly burst into bloom.

Arkoi

The largest of a cluster of islands north of Leipsoi, 11 nautical miles from Patmos. The harbor with its handful of inhabitants lies to the back of a fjord whose entrance is protected by other smaller islands. Arkoi has daily connections with Patmos in the summer.

Marathonisi

This small island with its beautiful sand beach lies opposite Arkoi.

Agathonisi

The northernmost island in the Dodecanese, 36 nautical miles from Patmos, whose small number of inhabitants are involved with fishing and animal husbandry. During the summer it has connections with Patmos twice a week.

The harbor and the picturesque shores of Leipsoi.

Practical Informations

When to go

The holiness of this island in combination with its healthy climate, its solid infrastructure and its important religious and historical sites makes it the ideal place for quiet holidays practically any time during the year.

The strongly indented coastline, low mountains, short distances and good roads create the right preconditions for those who like to walk. Anyone interested in combining the natural beauty of the island with the unique experience of a visit to the holy cave of the Apocalypse and the historic Monastery of St. John the Divine, will find spring the best season.

During the summer months the island is humming with life and there are more visitors who are seeking, besides a visit to the sights, the peace and quiet of the beaches and the picturesque bays of which Patmos offers so many.

All those who have made plans to visit the island at Easter will have an unforgettable experience as the Monastery of St. John the Divine celebrates the holy days with especial brilliance and religious intensity.

How to go

By ship: Patmos has connections with Piraeus, Rafina and Kavala all year round on large, modern passenger ships. From Piraeus the distance is 163 nautical miles and the trip takes 10-11 hours. Patmos also has year round connections with the islands of Kalymnos, Leros, Kos, Nisyros, Tilos, Rhodes, Symi, Karpathos and quite a number of the islands of the Cyclades such as Paros, Naxos, Mykonos, Syros and Tinos.

For more information contact the Harbor Master's Office at Piraeus, tel. (01) 4226000.

By ferry boat from Rafina on the Rafina-Aegean island line, Patmos has connections year round with Ayios Evstratios, Limnos, Lesbos, Samos, and Chios, ending at Kavala. During the summer there are also connections to Sigri on Lesbos and to Skyros. Information from the Harbor-Master's Office at Rafina (0244) 22300.

There are many buses of the KTEL line going from Athens to Rafina daily. The terminal is at the Pedion tou Areos and the trip takes an hour. Information in Athens, tel. 8210872.

On the ferry boats of the Aegean lines Patmos, Agathonisi and Arkoi are connected year round with Kalymnos, Leipsoi, Leros and Pythagoreio on Samos. Information at the Harbor-Master's Office of Patmos, tel. (0247) 31217, 31307.

From Patmos one can also take fast craft (hydrofoils) to most of the Dodecanesian islands and the eastern Aegean. Information at the agencies on Patmos, tel. (0247) 31217, 31307, 31205.

By Air: Patmos is served by the airports on Leros and Samos.

Where to stay

In recent times Patmos has had to respond to the demands of an ever-swelling flood of tourists. It has an adequate number of hotels and rooms to rent and is ready to welcome you.

Of course, if you are thinking of visiting the island in August (particularly around 15 August), or Easter then you should reserve your rooms before arrival. Those who prefer to spend their holidays in a tent will find an organized camping site at Meloi beach which is very near Skala.

Thus you will be able to combine the peace and quiet offered by this location with the bustle and entertainment of Skala.

If you are thinking of going to Patmos from

November to March you should telephone the office of tourist information at the Town Hall, tel. (0247) 31666.

Beaches

In addition to its religious character Patmos is also distinguished for its impressive cliffs and bays and its quiet and picturesque beaches. The most popular ones are at Kato Kambos, which is highly frequented and social and affords access to sea sports. Then there are Psili Ammos with its golden sand and Lambi with its superb colored pebbles.

There is also the beach at Groikos, protected from the wind by the islet of Tragonisi, and the beach at Kallikatzous with a conical rock at the tip of the cape as well as many others that can also serve you.

Transportation

The buses on the island have regular schedules all year round to the three settlements on the island, Chora, Skala and Kambos as well as the beaches at Groikos and Kato Kambos.

You can get information on exact times of departure from the Tourist office. There are also taxis and offices for the rental of cars and motorbikes.

Boat Service

During the summer, small boats leave daily from the harbor of Skala and go to the surrounding beaches, mainly Psili Ammos which cannot be reached by any other transport. You can also visit the neighboring island of Leipsoi with its marvelous beaches and the small islands of Arkoi and Agathonisi.

Useful Phone Numbers (0247)

Municipality of Patmos: 31235, 31058, 32278. **Police Station:** 31303, **OTE (Phone Company):** 31399, **DEH (Electic Company):** 31333, 31562, **Harbor Master's Office:** 31231, **Customs:** 31312, **Post Office:** 31316, **Hospital:** 31211, **Taxi Stand:** 31225, **Tourist Office:** 31666.

MONASTERIES:
Holy Monastery of St. John the Divine: tel. 31398. **Apocalypse:** 31234, **Evangelismos:** 31276, **Zoodochos Pigi:** 31256, **Ayia Ayion:** 31030. **Visiting Times:**
Holy Monastery of St. John the Divine:
Monday - Tuesday - Wednesday: 8 a.m.- 2 p.m. Thursday: 8 a.m. - 2 p.m. and 4 p.m. - 6 p.m. Friday - Saturday: 8 a.m. - 2 p.m.
Sunday: 8 a.m - 12 and 4 p.m. - 6 p.m.

HOTELS OF PATMOS

GRIKOS

GOLDEN SUN	B′	32318
ALEXANDROS	C′	31790
APOLAFSIS	C′	31380
GRIKOS	C′	31167
JOANNA	C′	31031
NIKOS	C′	32492
PANORAMA	C′	31209
PATMIAN HOUSE	C′	31180
PETRA	C′	31035
SILVER BEACH	C′	32652

KAMPOS

PATMOS PARADISE	B′	32624

MELOЇ

PORTO SCOUTARI	B′	33124

NETIES

PORTO MERICA	C′	32078

SKALA

ROMEOS	B′	34011
SKALA	B′	31343
ADONIS	C′	31103
ASTERI	C′	32465
BLUE BAY	C′	31165
BYZANCE	C′	31052
CAPTAINS HOUSE	C′	31793
CHRIS	C′	31403

DELFINI	C′	32080
EFI	C′	32500
GALINI	C′	31740
HELLINIS	C′	31275
KASTELI	C′	31361
MARIA	C′	31201
PLAZA	C′	31217
SUMMER	C′	31769
VILLA KASSANDRA	C′	31523
DIETHNES	D′	31357
SUNSET	D′	31411
KASTRO	D′	31554
AUSTRALIS	E′	31576

CAMPING PATMOS

MELOI	—	31821

Greek MYTHOLOGY

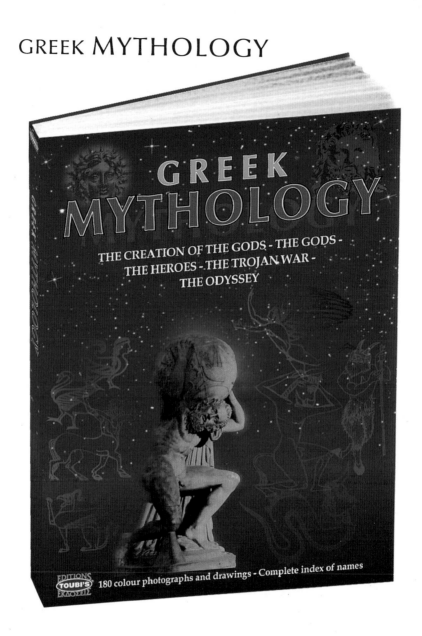

*T*his special edition has been designed to present the main
Greek myths. A work of considerable scope,
written in a simple and expressive language, it is accompanied
by 180 photographs and excerpts from ancient Greek literature.
Pages: 176, format: 17 × 24 cm